LEARNING ABOUT COINS

Please visit our web site at: www.garethstevens.com
For a free color catalog describing Gareth Stevens Publishing's list
of high-quality books and multimedia programs, call 1-800-542-2595 (USA)
or 1-800-387-3178 (Canada). Gareth Stevens Publishing's fax: (414) 332-3567.

Library of Congress Cataloging-in-Publication Data

Williams, Rozanne Lanczak.
   Learning about coins / written by Rozanne Lanczak Williams; photographed by Michael Jarrett. — North American ed.
     p. cm. — (I can do math)
   Summary: A group of children demonstrates how to count pennies, nickels, dimes, and quarters.
   ISBN 0-8368-4110-7 (lib. bdg.)
   1. Counting—Juvenille literature. 2. Coins, American—Juvenille literature. (1. Counting. 2. Coins. 3. Money.)
  I. Jarrett, Michael, 1956- ill. II. Title. III. Series.
QA113.W557   2004
513.2'11—dc22   2003066198

This North American edition first published in 2004 by
Gareth Stevens Publishing
A World Almanac Education Group Company
330 West Olive Street, Suite 100
Milwaukee, WI 53212 USA

Original copyright © 1995 by Creative Teaching Press, Inc.
First published in the United States in 1995 as *The Magic Money Box*
in the Learn to Read -- Read to Learn Math Series by Creative Teaching
Press, Inc., P.O. Box 2723, Huntington Beach, CA 92647-0723.

Gareth Stevens series editor: Dorothy L. Gibbs
Gareth Stevens series designer: Kami M. Koenig

Printed in the United States of America

2 3 4 5 6 7 8 9 09 08 07 06 05

LEARNING ABOUT COINS

Written by Rozanne Lanczak Williams
Photographed by Michael Jarrett

I CAN
+ DO
MATH

Gareth Stevens Publishing
A WORLD ALMANAC EDUCATION GROUP COMPANY

This is a magic money box!
Come and see the
tricks you can do.

5

In go five pennies.

Out comes a nickel!

In go five pennies and one nickel.

Out comes a dime! 9

In go two dimes and one nickel.

Out comes a quarter!

12

In go five nickels.

Out comes a quarter!

14 **In go five dimes.**

Out come two quarters! 15

In go two quarters.

Out comes a half-dollar! 17

And now . . .

In go twenty pennies, one nickel,
five dimes, and one quarter.

19

Out comes a dollar!

MATH QUIZ (answers on page 24)

1. If you put these coins in the magic money box, what comes out?

A. two nickels

B. one dime and three nickels

C. one quarter, one dime, one nickel,

and ten pennies

22

2. Which group of coins would make a quarter come out of the magic money box?

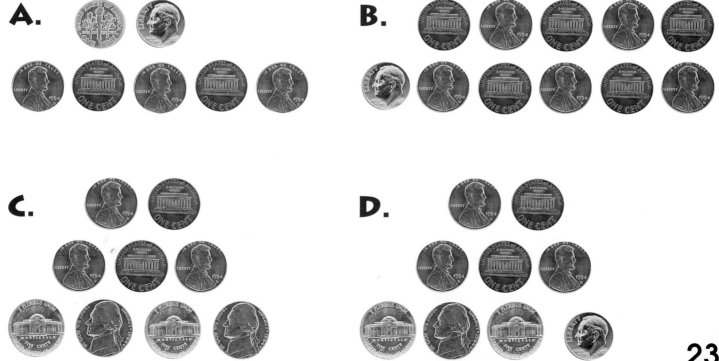

A.

B.

C.

D.

Answers:

1. A. a dime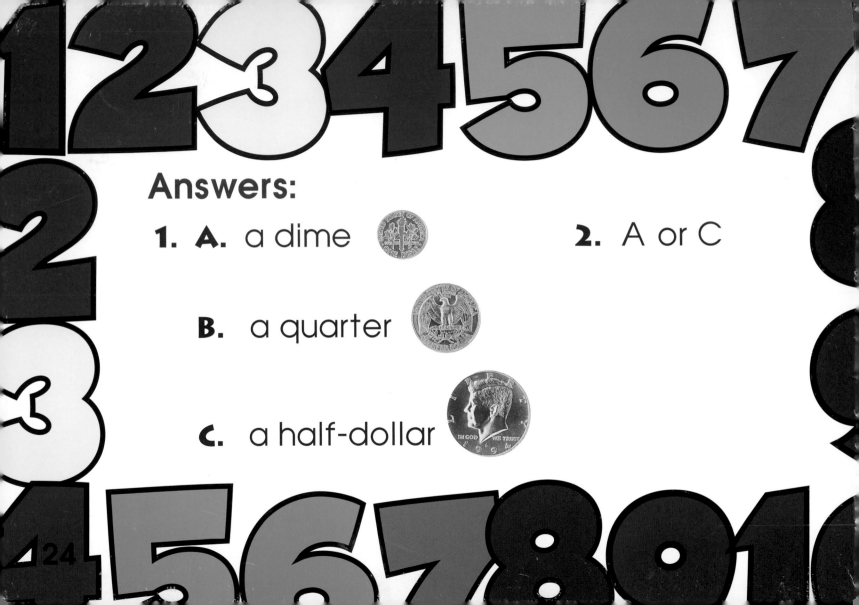

B. a quarter

C. a half-dollar

2. A or C